KEY STAGE 2
Parents' Guide
English Homework

Authors
Paul Beeston
Mike Waterhouse

Consultants
Penny Coltman
Valerie Mitchell

Series editor
Alwyn Morgan

EDUCATIONAL

Every effort has been made to trace copyright holders and to obtain their permission for the use of copyright material. The authors and publishers will gladly receive information enabling them to rectify any error or omission in subsequent editions.

First published 1998
Reprinted 1998

Letts Educational, Schools and Colleges Division,
9-15 Aldine Street, London W12 8AW
Tel: 0181 740 2270
Fax: 0181 740 2280

© Text – Letts Educational
© Illustrations – Letts Educational

Design by Charles Design Associates
Project Management – Rosine Faucompré
Illustration by Maxine Handley

All our rights reserved. No part of this publication may be reproduced, stored in a retrieval system, or transmitted, in any form or by means, electronic, mechanical, photocopying, recording or otherwise, without prior permission of Letts.

British Library Cataloguing-in-Publication Data.
A CIP record for this book is available from the British Library

ISBN 1 84085 023 X

Printed in Great Britain by Ashford Colour Press

Letts Educational is the trading name of BPP [Letts Educational] Ltd

CONTENTS

Introduction	2
Key Stage 2	5
Helping your Child to Spell	8
The Literacy Hour	10
Basic Word List 1	11
Basic Word List 2	14
Basic Word List 3	17
Word Groups	20
Recommended Book List	22
Activities	27
In the home ...	28
At the shops ...	31
On holiday ...	34
Writing letters ...	37
Glossary	38

INTRODUCTION

This guide will help parents and carers to support their children's English school work. It is important that home and school work together to make sure that developing literacy skills becomes a part of everyday life. It should not be seen simply as something to be taught by a teacher at school. Parents and carers are important educators of their children too.

Opportunities to stimulate English language work are all around us, everyday, all of the time. With your help, your child will benefit considerably from all the learning opportunities that you can provide, in the home, down the road, out shopping or on holiday. This will assist in building on their progress at school.

In all of these situations, talking, asking questions, involving your child in decision making, and providing praise and encouragement will help your child to enjoy making progress in English.

In this guide you will find a range of information that will be of help to you, including suggested reading books, spelling lists, and ideas for practical ways in which you can actively play a very important part in your child's education.

REMEMBER TO...

- Always encourage and be positive – provide plenty of praise.

- Be patient – give your child time to think and talk. Don't expect too much too soon.

- Match the speed and amount of work to the child's ability – little and often is the best way forward. Build on what they already know.

- Do not get upset if they do not finish a task.

REMEMBER TO...

- Accept that children may forget things. We all do.

- Use open ended questions, not closed ones. For example, "Why do you think that shop is called 'Ring-a- Roses'?" rather than, "What is that shop called?" Other useful questions may include – Tell me how…? What is happening now…? I wonder why…? How do they do that? etc.

- From time to time you may wish to offer small incentives and rewards.

- Talk about their successes.

KEY STAGE 2

ENGLISH AND THE NATIONAL CURRICULUM

The National Curriculum is organised into four Key Stages.

- Key Stage 1 – age range 5–7.
- Key Stage 2 – age range 7–11.
- Key Stage 3 – age range 11–14.
- Key Stage 4 – age range 14–16.

For each subject there is a Programme of Study which describes what is to be taught. The Programme of Study for English is divided into three sections. These sections are:

Speaking and Listening

To develop speaking and listening skills, pupils are taught to use standard English. They clarify and express their ideas, and are expected to adapt their speech to suit different audiences and circumstances. They should listen, understand and respond appropriately to others.

Reading

Children should be taught to read accurately, fluently and with understanding. They should read and study a wide range of texts, including traditional English literature and writing from other cultures.

Writing

Within this area, children should be taught accurate punctuation, correct spelling and legible handwriting. They should also learn how to improve the content of their writing. This includes developing ideas and communicating meaning. It also involves developing a wide-ranging vocabulary, learning to write for different audiences, and learning to write grammatically correct sentences.

MONITORING PROGRESS

Another part of the National Curriculum document describes different levels of achievement or attainment in English. There are eight levels of attainment. A good GCSE pass in English is level 8.

As children enter Key Stage 2, the majority of them will be working at Level 2. Some children will have reached Level 3, and others who are having difficulties in particular areas may still be working at Level 1.

Children continue to make progress through the levels, so that by the end of Key Stage 2, a child of average ability will be working at Level 4. More able children may be working at Level 5 and others may still be working at Level 3.

Your child's teacher will be able to give you more information about the different levels of attainment.

Attainment is assessed continuously during children's time at school to keep a check on their progress.

At the end of each Key Stage teachers use evidence from classroom work to decide which level best describes each child's achievements.

Children also take National Tests in reading and writing. You will be given a written record to show both the teacher's assessment of your child and their individual National Test result.

KEY STAGE 2

The English Test is in four parts:

- **Reading Comprehension**
  Children are given a ten page booklet. After they have read this, they answer questions which show their understanding of the text.

- **Spelling**
  The children are asked to write down the spelling of twenty words.

- **Handwriting**
  Children copy out a short set passage in their best handwriting.

- **Writing**
  Children plan and write either a short story or a piece of non-narrative writing, such as a letter, speech or information leaflet.

HELPING YOUR CHILD TO SPELL

The word lists on pages 11 to 19 are a guide to the words it would be helpful for your child to learn. He or she may also bring spellings home from school.

How can you help your child learn these spellings?

One way of learning spellings commonly encouraged in schools is the READ SAY COVER WRITE CHECK method.

READ

Read the word to your child. As you do this, look for any ways of helping them to remember the spelling. Is it part of a word group? Are there smaller words contained in it? e.g. 'sand' in the word 'sandwich'.

SAY

Ask your child to repeat the word out loud.

COVER

Cover the word so it cannot be seen.

SPELLING

WRITE
Your child now writes the word from memory.

CHECK
Check together to see if it is spelled correctly. If it is, go on to another word. If it is not, discuss how much of the attempt was correct and which parts need to be changed.

WRITE

CHECK

Remember to make the learning sessions fun. Use a variety of word lists to encourage your child. It may be helpful to use the spellings that your child is working on in school as a starting point. Don't try too many spellings in one go ... do not criticise your child for a wrong answer ... and keep smiling.

That was a good effort – well done!

THE LITERACY HOUR

From September 1998 it is recommended that schools set aside a minimum of an hour a day for teaching literacy.

During each literacy hour children will read with the teacher some text, which may be a story, a poem or a piece of information. The children will then carry out a variety of activities which might include, for example, talking about what the text means, discussing how it is put together, or thinking about the audience for whom it was written. The text might then be used as a starting point for a children's writing activity.

Children will also look at the sentences used in the text. For example, they might look at the way 'connecting words' such as 'although', 'however', 'because' or 'but' are used in sentences. Having made a collection of these words, children might be asked to use them in sentences of their own.

Finally, the text will be used as the basis for some spelling or vocabulary work. Children might use a dictionary to look up any new words and use the words in sentences of their own, and practise spelling them.

The activities carried out each day will vary, but the basic structure of work at text, sentence and word level will be common to each literacy hour.

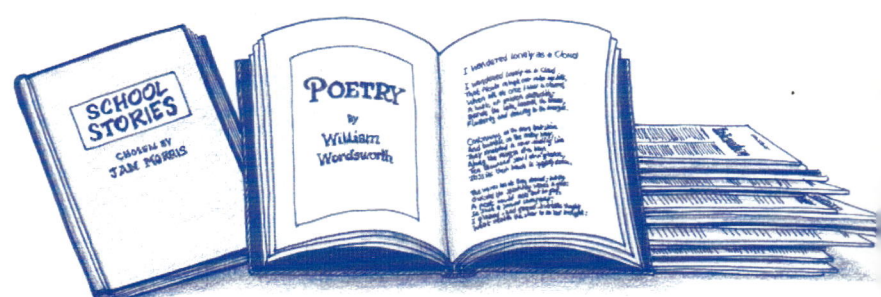

WORD LIST

BASIC WORD LIST 1

This is a list of 100 common words which make up the bulk of the reading matter for children at Key Stage 2. Two further lists show the next 200 most frequently used words.

You can use lists like these for checking that your child can read and say each word. Once they are happily reading the words they can then practise the spelling.

These words form the basic vocabulary which most children will have already encountered at Key Stage 1. It is helpful to check that children are confident in the use of these words as this will support their progress in both reading and spelling.

Remember to concentrate on reading each word aloud, to reinforce the sequence of sounds, before writing the spelling. Take a few at a time.

As children use different strategies to learn spellings, it may be helpful to group the words in a variety of different ways.

- <u>Lists that have similar visual patterns:</u> play, played, playing, before, began
- <u>Lists that are linked to speech:</u> said, called, replied
- <u>Lists that are linked to positions:</u> up, down, above, below, behind.

	Reading	Spelling
a		
about		
after		
all		
an		
and		
are		

	Reading	Spelling
as		
at		
back		
be		
because		
bed		
big		
but		

WORD LIST

	Reading	Spelling		Reading	Spelling
called			I		
came			if		
can			in		
come			into		
could			is		
dad			it		
day			like		
did			little		
do			made		
dog			man		
door			me		
down			mum		
for			my		
get			name		
go			next		
going			night		
good			no		
got			not		
had			of		
has			off		
have			on		
he			once		
her			one		
him			our		
his			out		
home					
house					

WORD LIST

	Reading	Spelling		Reading	Spelling
people			two		
put			up		
ran			very		
said			was		
saw			we		
school			went		
see			were		
she			what		
so			when		
some			will		
that			with		
the			would		
their			you		
them					
then					
there					
they					
time					
to					
took					

BASIC WORD LIST 2

Once a child has mastered most or all of the first 100 common words, it may be useful to move onto the next 100, listed here. Once again, the emphasis should be on reading first, then spelling.

Don't forget to make learning fun, and don't make the sessions too long.

Here are a few suggestions: Help children to memorise spelling patterns. For example, drawing a picture of an ear and arranging all the words with 'ear' (e.g. 'year') around it, can help with visual memory.

Make a set of word cards based on the spellings you wish to practise. Use the cards to play:

Snap Children say 'snap' if two words have the same ending. (Cat-hat = 'snap')

Picking up pairs Children turn over the cards. When they find two words which have something in common they may keep them as a 'pair' but only if they are able to explain their reasoning, e.g. both have the same initial letter, or same letter string.

Hunt and Point (played in pairs) Lay all the word cards face up. Call out an initial, end or middle sound. Children then race to point to an appropriate word card by placing a finger on it. The winner keeps the card.

	Reading	Spelling
am		
again		
another		
asked		
away		
bad		
balloon		

	Reading	Spelling
black		
blue		
boy		
brother		
by		
car		
castle		
cat		

WORD LIST

	Reading	Spelling		Reading	Spelling
children			king		
Christmas			know		
didn't			lived		
don't			long		
dragon			look		
eat			looked		
eyes			lots		
fell			make		
fire			more		
first			morning		
food			mother		
found			nice		
friend			now		
friends			oh		
from			old		
garden			opened		
gave			or		
giant			other		
girl			outside		
give			over		
gone			park		
hair			play		
heard			played		
help			playing		
here			red		
how			room		
just			round		

WORD LIST

	Reading	Spelling		Reading	Spelling
shop			walk		
sister			walked		
sleep			want		
something			water		
started			way		
story			well		
take			where		
tea			white		
things			who		
think			witch		
this			yes		
thought			your		
three					
through					
told					
too					
tree					
upon					
us					

BASIC WORD LIST 3

	Reading	Spelling
above		
across		
almost		
along		
also		
always		
animals		
any		
around		
baby		
before		
began		
being		
below		
better		
between		
birthday		
both		
brother		

	Reading	Spelling
brought		
can't		
change		
clothes		
coming		
different		
does		
during		
earth		
every		
father		
first		
follow		

WORD LIST

	Reading	Spelling		Reading	Spelling
goes			often		
great			only		
half			own		
happy			paper		
head			place		
high			pull		
important			push		
inside			right		
jump			second		
knew			seen		
lady			should		
laugh			show		
leave			small		
light					
love					
many					
might					
much					
must					
near					
never					
number					

WORD LIST

	Reading	Spelling
sometimes		
sound		
still		
stopped		
such		
suddenly		
sure		
swimming		
these		
those		
today		
together		
tries		
turn		
under		
until		
used		
watch		
which		
while		

	Reading	Spelling
whole		
why		
window		
with		
without		
woke		
word		
work		
world		
write		
year		
young		

Knowledge of these 300 words will give your child a good start in reading and spelling, though the average pupil will know many more words by the time they finish Key Stage 2 at the age of 11.

WORD GROUPS

Children should be encouraged to look for letter patterns in words from the moment they start reading. In addition to becoming familiar with the first 300 words, it is also helpful for children to look at lists which emphasise letter patterns in spelling.

These could include:
Lists that emphasise a particular letter string (examples below) -ight, -eight.

Lists of words that have the same prefix or suffix (examples below) tele-, -tion.

Some children also enjoy working with words which are linked by a theme:
wheel, brakes, engine, tyres, gears.
injection, operation, medicine, hospital, nurse.
saddle, bridle, hooves, stirrup, jodhpurs.

-ight words	light, sight, bright, fight, fright, tight, slight, might.
-or words	doctor, visitor, motor, horror, junior.
-eigh words	eight, weigh, weight, freight, neighbour.
-dge words	hedge, wedge, edge, bridge, ridge, midge.
-age words	page, cage, bandage, cottage, cabbage.
-ar words	vinegar, dollar, popular, jaguar, polar.
tele- words	television, telephone, telescope, telepathy.
-ible words	terrible, horrible, impossible, sensible, invisible.
-ure words	puncture, furniture, capture, overture, temperature.
-ea words	weather, leather, breath, breakfast, thread.
-tion words	mention, station, attention, ration, addiction.

WORD GROUPS

-ory words	factory, history, memory, story, directory, victory.
-ity words	activity, electricity, captivity, city, pity, capacity.
-ount words	count, mount, fountain, mountain.
-rash words	crash, brash, trash, thrash.
-ould words	could, would, should.
-mb words	climb, dumb, tomb, bomb.
-oast words	roast, toast, coast, boast.
-ong words	belong, strong, wrong, song, among.
-able words	cable, fable, stable, enable, disabled.
-ink words	shrink, drink, think, mink, brink.

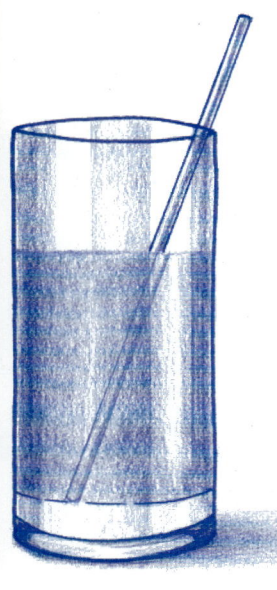

There are another 100 words here, but helping your child to read and spell these words will help with many more. An understanding of the similar spelling within word groups will help when attempting to spell an unknown word. It would be a good use of time to try to think of more word group patterns with your child.

Children will also need to know about compound words (two words joined to make one, like police-man or foot-ball). Work on compound words and prefixes and suffixes can be found in the Letts Homework Activity Books.

RECOMMENDED BOOK LIST

Hearing your child read

One way of helping your child is by encouraging him or her to read. During Key Stage 1 children are heard reading in school on a regular basis, and many will bring books home so that you can enjoy a book together.

However, at Key Stage 2, children may be heard reading less often. Consequently, encouraging reading as a leisure activity can be one of the best ways to improve a child's performance in English.

As you listen to your child reading, try to avoid interrupting too often. Allow time for new or difficult words to be deciphered. If your child finds a particular word very difficult, quietly supply it, and then return to it once the page is finished. This will prevent the enjoyment of the story being spoilt by too much disruption.

Once children are able to read fluently (e.g. can read a children's paperback novel with very little help), they prefer to read to themselves. Reading silently is much quicker than reading aloud, so you will be taking some of the pleasure from the book if you insist on hearing every word.

Wait until the end of the chapter is reached and then ask your child to tell you about the story. Invite your child to express opinions. What do you think is going to happen next? Why do you think the characters behaved as they did? Do they agree with decisions people made? Would they have written the story in quite the same way? It will be much easier for you to help your child in this way if you read at least some of the book yourself. Its enjoyment will then be a shared experience.

BOOK LIST

The book list below represents a very small selection of the many excellent books available in most good bookshops and libraries. The suggested year-groups are intended only as a guide. Involve your child in choosing books to read. Encourage them to talk about their interests. If they are enjoying a particular book at school, you could look for other books by the same author or with pictures by the same illustrator.

Look at the vocabulary level of the book when making or guiding a choice. Check that your child is going to understand the content of the story.

Encourage your child to sometimes make adventurous choices, trying new authors or types of story. Suggest occasional poetry books, or information texts.

REMEMBER
Even the most able readers will often appreciate books which have some illustration.

We all make bad choices sometimes! If your child is not enjoying a book, do not insist that it is read to the last page. Allow your child to recognise that its selection was a mistake, and to choose something else.

YEAR 3

Ahlberg, Janet and Allan	The Jolly Postman
	Ten in a Bed
Arkle, Phyllis	The Village Dinosaur
Avery, Gillian	Mouldy's Orphan
Briggs, Raymond	Jim and the Beanstalk
	Father Christmas Books
Burningham, John	Time to get out of the Bath, Shirley
Dahl, Roald	The Magic Finger
	George's Marvellous Medicine
Edwards, Dorothy	My Naughty Little Sister books
Geras, Adele	My Grandmother's Stories

BOOK LIST

Hughes, Shirley	Dogger
Hutchins, Pat	The House That Sailed Away
	The Mona Lisa Mystery
King-Smith, Dick	The Hodgeheg
	Sophie's Tom

YEAR 4

Ashley, Bernard	Dinner Ladies Don't Count
	I'm Trying to Tell You
Bawden, Nina	Keeping Henry
	Humbug
Brown, Jeff	Flat Stanley
Cleary, Beverley	Dear Mr. Henshaw
Cresswell, Helen	The Gift from Winklesea
Dahl, Roald	Matilda
Heide, Florence Parry	The Treehorn Books
	The Day of Ahmed's Secret
Hughes, Ted	The Iron Man
King, Clive	Stig of the Dump
Mahy, Margaret	The Great Piratical Rumbustification

YEAR 5

Ahlberg, Janet and Allan	Woof!
Byars, Betsy	TV Kid
	The Midnight Fox
	Eighteenth Emergency
Dahl, Roald	Danny, The Champion of the World
	Esio Trot

24

BOOK LIST

King-Smith, Dick	The Sheep-pig
	The Fox Busters
	Water Horse
	The Guard Dog
Lewis, C.S.	The Lion, the Witch and the Wardrobe
Mahy, Margaret	The Haunting
Pearce, Philippa	Lion at School
Townson, Hazel	The Great Ice-Cream Crime
	The Siege of Cobb Street School
White, E.B.	Charlotte's Web
Wynne Jones, Diana	Wild Robert

YEAR 6		
	Alcock, Vivian	The Haunting of Cassie Palmer
	Ashley, Bernard	Terry on the Fence
	Bawden, Nina	The Peppermint Pig

BOOK LIST

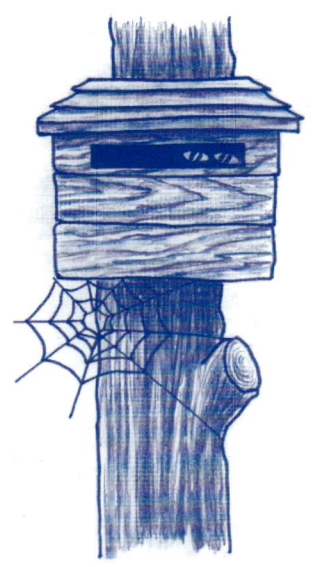

Blume, Judy	Superfudge
	It's not the End of the World
	Are you there, God?
	It's me Margaret
Byars, Betsy	Night Swimmers
Doherty, Berlie	Granny was a Buffer Girl
Fine, Ann	Bill's New Frock
Garner, Alan	Elidor
Kemp, Gene	The Turbulent Term of Tyke Tiler
	Gowie Corby Plays Chicken
Layton, George	The Fib and Other Stories
Lively, Penelope	The Ghost of Thomas Kemp
Mark, Jan	Feet and Other Stories
	The Dead Letter Box
	Thunder and Lightnings
	Handles
Naughton, Bill	The Goalkeeper's Revenge
Needle, Jan	A Game of Soldiers
Pearce, Philippa	Tom's Midnight Garden
	A Dog So Small
Townson, Hazel	The Deathwood Letters

ACTIVITIES

The suggested activities in this section provide ways to help you improve your child's English. They aim to make learning fun by making it a part of everyday life.

The activities include a range of tasks, some of which you may already be familiar with. Equally, an activity which you use may be missing from this brief guide. That does not mean you are doing something wrong!

The most important consideration, whatever you attempt to do, is to make it different from what happens at school. Do not say, 'Let us do some English activities.' Instead, make the activities part of normal family life. If the child does not enjoy taking part, change the activity. Children learn most effectively when they are motivated and interested. Also remember not to make the activity too lengthy. Look for signs of tiredness or boredom, and stop. You can always try again tomorrow

ACTIVITIES

In the home ...

- Discuss shared TV programmes. Talk about the 'plot', the 'characters' and the 'setting'. Introduce these terms as appropriate, and don't expect too deep an understanding of the programmes initially.

- Encourage the reading of newspapers. Begin with the things which young children will enjoy. Often papers have children's sections, and the TV page is usually interesting for children. Leave the newspapers open at the fashion and sports pages to encourage your child to browse before they are capable of reading complex text. Discuss the pictures with them. This will get them used to handling newspapers.

- If an interest is shown in newspapers, develop it by talking about things such as what item mentioned in the advertisements could be bought for £50, or which car they would choose if they had a budget of £2000.

ACTIVITIES

In the home ...

- Many children enjoy pop music. Try to listen to it with them (this can be difficult!). Talk about the lyrics. Can you make up your own words to a song?

- Talk about major news items. Young children may sympathise with people affected by misfortune, and may be able to give opinions on clear-cut issues such as capital punishment.
  Remember that it is the discussion and thinking which are important, even if you do not agree with their views.

- Comics and magazines can be useful. Talk about characters and storylines. Children who are not keen on writing might enjoy producing a comic-style picture story.

ACTIVITIES

In the home ...

- Scrap books can be popular. Perhaps a favourite sports team or pop star can provide the stimulus for a child to look at (and cut up) newspapers and magazines.

- Word games can improve vocabulary. Obvious ones are:
  - **Scrabble**: a junior version is also available, but many children can cope with the normal version. Give them a chance – double their scores every time.
  - **Boggle**: a spelling game using dice.
  - **Pictionary**: this develops children's vocabulary through picture work.
  - **Hangman**: can be played anywhere.
  - **Call My Bluff**: it can be fun to make up 'Call My Bluff' type questions with the use of a dictionary.
  - **Blockbusters**: is always popular with children.
  - **Charades** or '**Give Us a Clue**': encourage the use of drama skills.

ACTIVITIES

ACTIVITIES

At the shops ...

- Talk about advertising. Why are some slogans easy to remember? Which colours are used to advertise different products?

- Look at cans containing food and drink. What information can be read on a can? You may wish to set a task to find which foods came from a particular country, e.g. Spain. This may make the visit to the supermarket more enjoyable for your child. Perhaps a new label for a food container could be designed.

- Look out for interesting shop names – hairdressers and florists often have very unusual titles. Talk about the different names for shops. Does your child know what a grocery or a hardware shop is in these days of multi-purpose supermarkets?

ACTIVITIES

At the shops ...

- Look out for deliberate mistakes in shop and business names. You might see, for example, a business which uses lower case letters for the beginnings of its name, or a spelling mistake such as 'sox' for socks, 'U' for you, or even 'tacsi' for taxi! Finding the mistake, and talking about it, reinforces what should be there.

- Estate agents. Stop and look at their window displays and look at the advertisements in the papers. Can you write an advertisement for your house?

ACTIVITIES

At the shops ...

- Talk about the words used to describe places in the travel agents. Involve your child in the choice of holiday. Give them access to the brochures so they can read the information themselves.

- Asking a child to visit a local, safe shopping area can help develop confidence in speaking. Giving a shopping list, either when you are with the child or when they are with friends, provides much-needed reading practice. Encourage your child to help you to write your list, or their own!

Can I have a red cricket ball please?

ACTIVITIES

On holiday ...

- Share your holiday plans with your children. In a busy household it is sometimes difficult to find time to talk, and an annual holiday with the possibility of long journeys spent in each other's company can be a great opportunity for sharing time together.

- Look at place names. Look for similarities (BlackPOOL, LiverPOOL) and look for words within place names (SCARborough, ScarboROUGH).

- Use car number plates for word games (good for long, boring motorway journeys). Try to make words from the letters on a number plate. For example, PRH can give PeRcH, or apPRoacH, or PeRisH. Take it in turns to see who can make the longest word.

ACTIVITIES

On holiday...

- When on a motorway, look out for the towns/cities mentioned on vans and lorries. You might see who can find the most towns, who can find a town beginning with different letters of the alphabet, or you might ask who can see first the name of a city you are approaching.

- If you are on a cross-country journey in Britain, away from the motorways, look out for pub names and play 'Legs'. In this game, take turns to spot a pub name, and score the number of legs in the name. For example, 'The Duke of York' would score 2, 'The Black Bull' would score 4, 'The Crown and Anchor' would score 0. For a pub like 'The Coach and Horses' or 'The Hare and Hounds' where there is an indefinite number of legs, the score awarded is 20. This game helps the child to read signs, but also gives younger children a chance, because pubs often have pictures as well as their names on their signs.

- Use atlases and road maps to talk about your route. Let the children practise using the index or contents and help them try to read the place names. They will be able to suggest routes at a fairly early age.

ACTIVITIES

On holiday...

- Write a diary or account of your holiday. Children may treasure such accounts for years, as it is like having a reading book in which they feature. Make it a joint activity. Encourage them to write in or illustrate the account and to include tourist information leaflets.

- Use games. Hangman can be played anywhere, and I-Spy is even easier to play. For young children the normal game will be appropriate, and will help with initial sounds. For older children, try making it an 'adjective' I-Spy, where the answers will be adjectives such as red, dull, old, untidy etc. Use 'noun phrases' – 'I Spy with my little eye something beginning with BBD' might be Big Black Dog!

ACTIVITIES

Writing letters ...

- Encourage children to write letters, whether it is to thank Granny for her Christmas present, or to enter a TV or newspaper competition. The book 'Free Stuff for Kids' (ISBN 1850 15701 4) published by Exley Publications has lots of suggestions for writing to companies who are happy to give away free samples – a real encouragement to write letters!

The Coach House
Meadow Lane
Leatherhead
Surrey KT4 5XL

Dear Sir,
I am very interested in the of products
your company produc

Have fun ...

GLOSSARY

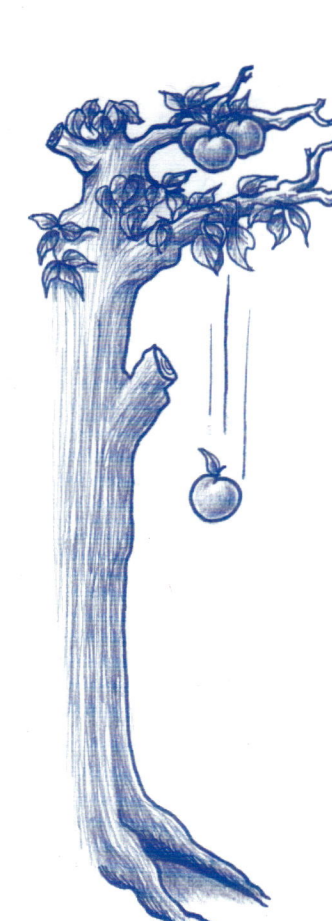

This list is intended to help understanding of the terms used in the Key Stage 2 English Homework Activity Book.

Acrostic
A type of poem where the first letter of each line spells out what the poem is about if one reads down the lines. An example is as follows:
> **J**oyful birds singing
> **U**nder green tree canopies
> **N**ights of soft darkness
> **E**xplode into a musical sunrise.

Adjective
A word which describes a noun. For example, a **pleasant** boy, a **new** car, a **red** apple.

Adverb
A word which tells you how, when or where an action happened. For example, the boy ran **quickly**, the car left **later**, the apple fell **down**.

Apostrophe
The small comma placed at letter height ('). It can be an *apostrophe or letters of omission* to show that a letter or letters have been missed out (**can't**) or an *apostrophe of possession* used to show that something belongs to something or someone else (**the boy's coat**).

Character
A person in a story, often an imaginary figure.

GLOSSARY

Cinquain
A type of poetry based on each line having a certain number of syllables (line 1 = 2; line 2 = 4; line 3 = 6; line 4 = 8; and line 5 = 2). An example is as follows:

> *Listen*
> *With faint dry sound*
> *Like steps of passing ghosts*
> *The leaves, frost crisped break from the trees*
> *And fall.*

November Nights by Adelaide Crapsey

Chronological Writing
Writing which starts at the beginning and follows through the normal time scale, telling one thing after another.

Cloze Procedure
A means of assessing how well a pupil understands a passage by missing out every fifth or tenth word, so that the pupil has to work out a suitable word to fill each space.

Comprehension
Understanding what has been read. Pupils are assessed in reading at the end of their primary education by means of a comprehension test. The questions set may be *literal,* where the information needed to answer the question is in the writing on the page, and it simply needs finding. Another type of question is *inferential,* where the pupil has to work out the answer from what has been read, as the passage does not actually give the answer.

GLOSSARY

Conjunction
A word which joins two sentences together. Examples are **and**, **but**, **so**, **although**, and **when**. These are also called connectives.

Connective
See *Conjunction*.

Contraction
A shortened word like **can't** or **don't**. See also *Apostrophe*.

Drafting
Making a rough attempt at a piece of writing which will be changed and improved on before a final copy is presented.

In many schools, a special 'Drafting' or 'Planning' book is used for this work, and pupils will be expected to use this process for most of their writing in English lessons.

Fable
A short story with a message or moral, such as Aesop's Fables.

Fiction
Writing, such as stories, that is based on imagination rather than fact.

GLOSSARY

Haiku
A type of short poem with 17 syllables, originally from Japan. Usually the first line contains five syllables, the second contains seven syllables, and the final line contains five syllables. An example is as follows:

> *Rain drums on the pane*
> *And runs down, wavering the*
> *World into a dream*
>
> J.W. Hackett

Imaginative Writing
Writing where the pupil uses his or her imagination to make the reader interested in the content.

Inferential Questions
See *Comprehension*.

Key Stage 2
This is the period of schooling which caters for 7 to 11 year olds. It used to be called the Junior years.

Limerick
A five lined poem which starts 'There was a young/old man/woman from..."

Literal Questions
See *Comprehension*.

Lower Case Letters
Normal or small letters (as opposed to capitals), e.g. a, b, c, d, e etc.

Narrative Writing
Writing which tells a story.

National Curriculum
See pages 5–7 of this booklet.

GLOSSARY

Non-fiction
Factual writing, about real people or events.

Noun
A word which is the name of a person or thing. For example, **boy**, **car** or **apple**. A Proper Noun is a specific name such as **Michael**, **Paris**, or **Fiat**.

Paragraph
A group of sentences all written about the same topic.

Plural
More than one thing. For example, **two boys**, **some cars**, **many apples**.

Prefix
Letters added to the beginning of a word to change its meaning. For example DISappear, WITHhold, PREcaution.

Pronoun
A word which stands in the place of a noun. Examples are **he**, **they**, **it**.

Proof-reading
Checking over writing to make sure that there are no errors in spelling or punctuation.

Pun
Play on words or the humorous use of words to suggest different meanings.

Punctuation
Full stops, commas, speech marks, question marks, exclamation marks and dashes that help our writing to be understood.

GLOSSARY

Reference Skills
The ability to look for information or facts in books, libraries, computers and other sources.

Sequencing
Putting into the correct order, usually the order in which events occurred.

Setting
The place where a story happens.

Simile
An expression or saying such as **as steady as a rock**, or **as busy as a bee**.

Singular
A single thing. For example, **a boy**, **one car**, **an apple**.

Speech Marks
The marks ("and") which are used to show where someone is speaking in a piece of writing. They are also called Inverted Commas.

Subject
The word or words in the sentence which carry out the action. For example, **the boy** ran down the street.

Suffix
A suffix is a group of letters added to the end of a word which can change the word's meaning. For example, moveMENT, careLESS, playER.

Syllable
Part of a word that contains a single sound and is pronounced as one unit, e.g. small is one syllable, smaller is two syllables.

GLOSSARY

Text
The written word.

Upper Case Letters
Capital letters, as used at the start of sentences or special names, e.g. A, B, C, D, E etc.

Verb
An action or 'doing' word, for example, **run**, **leave**, **fall**.

Vocabulary
The range of words used in speech or writing.

Word Attack Skills
The ways in which readers work out what words say. These skills include sounding out the word by the letters it contains, or guessing what the word must be by looking at the other words in the sentence and trying to make sense of it.

YOUR NOTES

YOUR NOTES